TEEN
PROBLEMS

TEEN SUICIDE

By Mary Quirk

ReferencePoint Press®

San Diego, CA

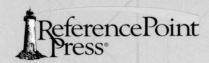

For more information, contact:
ReferencePoint Press, Inc.
PO Box 27779
San Diego, CA 92198
www.ReferencePointPress.com

Content Consultant: Lillian Polanco-Roman, PhD, Licensed Clinical Psychologist

LIBRARY OF CONGRESS CATALOGING-IN-PUBLICATION DATA

Names: Quirk, Mary, author.
Title: Teen suicide / Mary Quirk.
Description: San Diego : ReferencePoint Press, 2021. | Series: Teen problems | Includes
  bibliographical references and index. | Audience: Grades 10-12
Identifiers: LCCN 2020003711 (print) | LCCN 2020003712 (eBook) | ISBN 9781682829677
  (hardcover) | ISBN 9781682829684 (eBook)
Subjects: LCSH: Teenagers--Suicidal behavior--Juvenile literature. | Suicide--Prevention--
  Juvenile literature. | Teenagers--Mental health--Juvenile literature.
Classification: LCC HV6546 .Q57 2021 (print) | LCC HV6546 (eBook) | DDC 362.280835--
  dc23
LC record available at https://lccn.loc.gov/2020003711
LC eBook record available at https://lccn.loc.gov/2020003712

CONTENTS

SUICIDE IN THE MEDIA

Seventeen-year-old Hannah Baker's suicide generated more than 600,000 news stories and 11 million tweets. A fictional character in the Netflix series *13 Reasons Why*, based on the 2007 young adult novel, Hannah had experienced loneliness, sexual assault, cyberbullying, family financial troubles, feeling like a burden to her family and friends, and depression during the year leading up to her death. Any one of her experiences creates a risk factor for suicide.

The suicide of Hannah Baker stirred serious debate. Viewers argued about the media depiction of suicide in teens and its potential for copycat suicides. *Copycat suicides* refers to one or more suicides related to real or fictional accounts of suicide in the media. People on one side of the debate said the series glorified the act of suicide in a way that promotes it. Others felt the series raised awareness about suicide. Mental health experts thought the story inaccurately showed the causes

TV shows and movies that show teen suicide can have positive and negative effects. They may spread awareness, or they may increase copycat suicides.

of suicide. They said the show emphasized traumatic events as a source and did not put enough focus on Hannah's underlying mental health issues. People also debated whether the show discouraged those struggling with suicidal urges from seeking help, since Hannah sought help several times from school counselors and the principal, but they did not assist her.

Katherine Langford played Hannah in *13 Reasons Why*. The show's depiction of suicide has sparked controversy.

The series opens with Hannah's voiceover followed by the discovery of a box with thirteen audiocassette tapes—an audio diary—in which Hannah discusses the thirteen reasons for her suicide. In its original release, the first season of *13 Reasons Why* ended with a graphic depiction of her death during a three-minute scene. In July 2019, two years after the series launched and following requests from many experts, Netflix edited this scene. The updated version of the episode no longer shows Hannah's suicide. It ends with her parents finding her dead in the bathroom.

Was the release of *13 Reasons Why* linked to more suicides in the United States? The researchers for one study wrote,

"Specifically, excess suicides of approximately 15 percent occurred in the first month after the show's release in the main target group, 10- to 19-year-old individuals."[1] For this post-show period, researchers compared the expected number of suicides with the actual numbers of suicides. The difference they found represented excess suicides, or the occurrence of more suicides than would have been predicted. Additional research from other groups looking at suicide data nationally and locally confirmed an increase in suicides, specifically in this age group. But according to the US Centers for Disease Control and Prevention (CDC), suicide rates in this age group have been increasing since 2007.

In contrast, two studies found a positive impact during the first season, showing increased suicide awareness among teens. In the second season of the show, researchers confirmed a positive impact for students who watched the entire second season. The showrunners had responded to the criticism about the first season's problematic portrayal of suicide and followed public health guidelines for the second season.

However, the results were not all positive, according to the study's senior author, Dan Romer. Romer is the University of Pennsylvania Annenberg Public Policy Center's research director. "Although there's some good news about the effects of *13 Reasons Why*, our findings confirm concerns about the show's potential for adverse effects on vulnerable viewers," Romer said.[2]

"*13 Reasons Why* seemed to be particularly upsetting for young people who were already at a higher risk of suicide and who empathized with the main character, 17-year-old Hannah, who is bullied and sexually assaulted before deciding to end her life."

In 2017, the World Health Organization (WHO) updated its resource booklet *Preventing Suicide: A Resource for Media Professionals*. It says, "The media can play a significant role in either enhancing or weakening suicide prevention efforts."[3] The series *13 Reasons Why* demonstrates both sides of this complicated issue.

> "The media can play a significant role in either enhancing or weakening suicide prevention efforts."[3]
> **—World Health Organization**

Suicide is a complex and distressing problem around the world, with nearly 800,000 people dying from suicide every year. In 2016, more than 200,000 people from ages ten to twenty-nine died from suicide, according to the WHO. Because of the stigma associated with suicide, it is often not acknowledged by families as the cause of death. *Stigma* means being marked by shame, dishonor, or scandal. Addressing societal stigmas plays an important role in suicide prevention, according to the WHO:

Stigma, particularly surrounding mental disorders and suicide, means many people thinking of taking their own life or who have attempted suicide are not seeking help and are therefore not getting the help they need. The prevention of suicide has not been adequately addressed due to a lack of awareness of suicide as a major public health problem and the taboo in many societies to openly discuss it.[4]

> "The prevention of suicide has not been adequately addressed due to a lack of awareness of suicide as a major public health problem and the taboo in many societies to openly discuss it."[4]
>
> **—World Health Organization**

For the majority of teens in the twenty-first century, death is rare. Teens make up approximately 25 percent of the population in the United States, and only 2 percent of all deaths occur during adolescence. Suicide among teens is also a relatively rare event. However, from 2011 to 2017, suicide replaced homicide as the second leading cause of death in US teens and young adults. The first leading cause of death was unintentional injury, such as car accidents. From 1950 to 1990, the suicide rate in US teens ages fifteen to nineteen years increased 300 percent. Many factors have contributed to this increase, according to the CDC. Understanding the causes of this problem and identifying effective prevention strategies are important for the future. Since the 1990s, suicide rates have gone down and back up. There is hope that these rates can decrease again.

CHAPTER ONE

WHAT IS SUICIDE?

Public health organizations define suicide as death caused by a self-directed injury with intent to die. Suicidal ideation is when someone has thoughts of suicide. Suicidal behavior, or suicidality, can include anything from suicidal ideation, to making plans for suicide, to attempts at suicide. While suicide itself is not a mental disorder, it is often caused by underlying mental health issues such as depression, bipolar disorder, or substance use disorder. Some of the language currently used to describe suicide and suicidal behavior can reinforce dangerous stereotypes, misconceptions, and stigma. Stigma is a set of negative and often unfair beliefs held by society about something. It often is associated with feelings of shame. Suicide is often talked or written about in the media with the phrase "committed suicide." If someone attempts suicide and survives, the media might call it a "failed suicide attempt." Words matter when mental health professionals and the media talk about

The language surrounding suicide matters. Some phrases place blame on the victim.

suicide and suicide attempts, and this is why people should be mindful of the language they use to discuss suicide.

Word choice can help or hurt others when talking about suicide. Using words like *defective*, *insane*, or *crazy* to describe people with mental illness can be harmful. It treats them as inferior or insignificant, according to the American Association of Suicidology (AAS). The association states, "When inappropriate language is used, it may confirm fears of those struggling with suicidal thoughts that they are misunderstood, inadequate, or alone."[5] Some of the current language used to describe suicide is biased, and it may contribute to people keeping silent about suicidal thoughts or behavior and not seeking treatment to prevent suicide.

As the WHO explains in its guidelines for the media, "Don't use language which sensationalizes or normalizes suicide, or presents it as a constructive solution to problems."[6] Use of "commit/committed suicide" is an example of problematic terminology. The definition of the word *commit* in the Merriam-Webster online dictionary is accompanied by two examples of usage: "commit a crime" and "commit a sin."[7] These words "serve to criminalize or imply moral failings," according to the AAS.[8] Instead, the wording "died by suicide" is preferred usage.

"Don't use language which sensationalizes or normalizes suicide, or presents it as a constructive solution to problems."[6]

—*World Health Organization*

The AAS also warns against the phrase "cry for help." This wrongly suggests suicide was an attempt to get attention.

Suicide should also not be described as a selfish act. Finally, use of the phrase "failed attempt" is especially problematic as it implies that death equals success, experts say. When posting information about suicide online, check for harmful language before sharing it.

HISTORICAL, CULTURAL, AND LEGAL PERSPECTIVES

From the mid-thirteenth century until the mid-twentieth century, suicide was referred to as "self-murder," and it was considered a serious criminal offense in many Western countries. As of 2016, suicide was still illegal in twenty-five countries. In some cases, these laws on suicide stated that a person who died from suicide lost their right to a religious burial and surviving family members were not allowed to inherit their land or property. The property went to the government instead. Today, suicide and suicide attempts are no longer a crime in most countries. "Attitudes to suicidal behavior have changed over time and at different times in different places," said Professor Nav Kapur, head of research at Manchester University's Centre for Suicide Prevention.[9] Physician-assisted suicide is a topical example of changing attitudes on suicide. This refers to when a doctor helps a terminally ill patient's death by suicide if the patient requests it, usually by providing the terminally ill patient with drugs to self-administer. As of January 2020, many states and countries have passed legislation dealing with assisted suicide, both in favor of and against it.

A COMPLEX AND VEXING ISSUE

Today, teens can find themselves emotionally overwhelmed and in suicidal distress due to a web of psychological, environmental, and social factors. Understanding the factors that contribute to suicide can help to prevent it from happening in the future. According to the American Academy of Pediatrics (AAP), "More than 90 percent of adolescent suicide victims met criteria for a psychiatric disorder before their death. Immediate risk factors include agitation, intoxication, and a recent stressful life event."[10]

> "More than 90 percent of adolescent suicide victims met criteria for a psychiatric disorder before their death. Immediate risk factors include agitation, intoxication, and a recent stressful life event."[10]
>
> —*American Academy of Pediatrics*

It is also important to remember that the majority of teens with risk factors for suicide do not die by suicide. A definitive test for determining future suicidal behavior does not exist, according to the American Psychological Association (APA). However, experts have identified many risk factors for suicide. Risk factors are any individual, familial, and societal links that contribute to suicide risk. Some examples of risk factors for suicide include excessive alcohol use, family history of suicide, and limited access to mental health treatment. Along with risk factors, there are also protective factors that guard against suicide. Examples include a sense of connectedness and easy access to mental health treatment.

MENTAL FACTORS

In teens, major depression has been long acknowledged by experts as being strongly linked to suicide. In 2017, an episode of major depression that interfered with normal life activities affected an estimated 2.3 million youth ages twelve to seventeen in the United States, according to the National Institute of Mental Health (NIMH). In 2013, the

WHAT IS PSYCHOSIS?

Psychosis is strongly linked to suicidal behavior across multiple studies. In one study, researchers reported a seventy-fold increase in suicidal behavior among teens with psychosis. Psychologist Nev Jones of the University of South Florida is an expert on psychosis. Her experience with the disorder as a graduate student led her to conduct research about early psychosis. Mental health intervention during a first episode of psychosis is critical, according to Jones. Early intervention can help a young person stay connected to family, friends, school, and work, which relates to a better quality of life. In the United States, an estimated 100,000 people are diagnosed with psychosis each year.

Jones said,

Early psychosis symptoms can be very different from full-on psychosis symptoms. They are a lot subtler. I would feel certain stuff, like my hands were blending into the arms of a chair, or the ground was no longer solid. . . . The other health care folks kept asking me, 'Are you hearing voices?' It was subtle, so I couldn't say yes. My world felt very off, but I couldn't put my finger on why.

Quoted in Andy Steiner, "Nev Jones: First-Episode Psychosis Programs Help Young People Continue their Lives," MinnPost, *March 4, 2016,* www.minnpost.com.

APA updated their handbook for doctors to include more than twenty other mental illnesses that also carry a risk for suicide. These conditions include psychosis, anorexia nervosa, anxiety, schizophrenia, and post-traumatic stress disorder (PTSD).

Addiction to drugs or alcohol is also considered a mental illness, according to NIMH. *Substance use disorder* is the term used by mental health professionals. In the United States, millions of people have a substance use disorder. Having both a substance-use disorder and another co-occurring mental illness can make both conditions harder to treat and increase the risk for suicide. Mental health experts use the words *chronic* and *acute* to describe issues with drugs and alcohol. Chronic substance use refers to ongoing, daily use of the substance. Acute substance use means using excessive amounts in a short period.

"Acute alcohol use has been found to be associated with more than one-third of suicides and approximately 40 percent of suicide attempts."[11]
—*CDC's National Center for Injury Prevention and Control*

CDC's National Center for Injury Prevention and Control states, "Acute alcohol use has been found to be associated with more than one-third of suicides and approximately 40 percent of suicide attempts."[11]

Acute substance use means someone uses an excessive amount of alcohol or drugs. This increases someone's risk for suicide.

Another major risk factor for suicide is suicidal ideation or thoughts. Around 50 to 75 percent of youth suicide deaths are initial attempts. For those who do not die by suicide in the initial attempt, previous suicide attempts also represent a risk factor. According to NIMH,

Research suggests that people who attempt suicide may react to events, think, and make decisions differently than those who do not attempt suicide. These differences happen more often if a person also has a disorder such as depression, substance abuse, anxiety, borderline personality disorder, and psychosis.[12]

Every two years, the CDC conducts the Youth Risk Behavior Survey of high school students in ninth to twelfth grade across the United States. One of the questions on the survey asks if suicide had been attempted in the past year. Data from the 2017 survey of high school students show one or more attempted suicides by 7.4 percent of students in the year leading up to the survey. It is important to remember that a suicide attempt might not result in injury.

SOCIAL AND ENVIRONMENTAL FACTORS

Research on suicide also looks at the influences of social and physical factors, such as family dynamics, sexual identity, and stressful life events. According to the CDC's National Violent Death Reporting System, the factors for suicide deaths (excluding mental health disorders) from highest to lowest are as follows: 42 percent of those who died had a relationship problem, 29 percent had a crisis in the past or in the upcoming two weeks, 28 percent had problematic substance use, such as alcohol and drug use, 22 percent had a physical health problem, 16 percent had a financial problem, 9 percent had a criminal legal problem, and 4 percent had a loss of housing. These problems often overlapped, meaning the total added up to more than 100 percent. The CDC notes, "Data on mental health conditions and other factors are from coroner/medical examiner and law enforcement reports. It is possible that mental health

There are factors other than mental health disorders that cause suicide. One of the most common is relationship problems.

conditions or other circumstances could have been present and not diagnosed, known, or reported."[13]

Family history and dynamics can be factors in suicide and also protection from it. Teens have a higher risk of suicide if a parent has a mental illness, and family history of suicide or suicide attempts are associated with an even higher risk. From research studies in families, the suicide of a parent or sibling increased the risk of suicide 2.5-fold regardless of mental illness.

Family violence, such as physical or sexual abuse, is also linked to suicide. On the other hand, supportive relationships with family members, trusted adults, and friends can protect against suicide in teens.

Those who identify as lesbian, gay, bisexual, transgender, or queer/questioning (LGBTQ) are at a higher risk for suicide than those who are not part of the LGBTQ community. According to the 2017 CDC Youth Risk Behavior Survey, 47.7 percent of high schoolers who identified as gay, lesbian, and bisexual had considered attempting suicide in the year prior to being surveyed. Further, 31.8 percent of students who were not sure of their sexual orientation had considered a suicide attempt, as opposed to 13.3 percent of heterosexual students. This trend continues with students who attempted suicide. In the same study, 23 percent of gay, lesbian, and bisexual students reported having attempted suicide in the year prior to the study. The numbers were 14.3 percent of students not sure of their sexual orientation and 5.4 percent of heterosexual students. The Trevor Project is a national organization that provides crisis intervention and suicide prevention services for LGBTQ young people. It says, "Two key suicide risk factors are individual-level factors such as depression and experiences of stigma and discrimination, including anti-LGBT hostility, harassment, bullying, and family rejection."[14] Acceptance and support from individuals,

LGBTQ youth are at a higher risk for suicide than heterosexual youth. One factor may be that LGBTQ youth are bullied more often.

families, schools, employers, communities, and society for LGBTQ youth is critical to their general well-being.

INCREASING SUICIDE RATES

Since the beginning of the twenty-first century, suicide rates of teens by gender have changed. For example, one study found that from 1975 through 2007, male youth had significantly higher rates of suicide than female youth. From 2007 to 2016, female suicide deaths rose by 12.7 percent annually, compared to a 7.1 percent annual increase for male suicide deaths. This narrowed the gap between male and female suicide deaths.

The suicide rate among girls ages ten to fourteen years has increased. While they are lower than the rates of male youth, girls are more likely to think about and attempt suicide. Researchers point to growing evidence that the rising rate of suicide among girls is linked to the rise of social media and cyberbullying and that social media use might have a bigger impact on girls than boys for suicide risk. Professors Joan Luby and Sarah Kertz wrote about the impact of social media among girls in three research studies in an article for the *Journal of the American Medical Association (JAMA)*: "These findings suggest that increased social media use may have a more deleterious effect on girls, providing one potential explanation for why young girls may be increasingly vulnerable to suicidal thoughts and behaviors."[15]

In the United States, easier access to guns nationwide might also factor into the rising rates of suicide reported in almost every state. According to the Suicide Prevention Resource Center, taking measures to reduce access to guns, certain medications, or other potentially lethal items when a person is having suicidal

The suicide rate for girls has increased. This may be due to social media use and cyberbullying.

feelings or has recently attempted suicide is one of the most important steps in preventing suicide.

WARNING SIGNS

Mental health experts distinguish between risk factors and warning signs for suicide. While risk factors are familial or societal links that contribute to suicide risk, warning signs are specific behaviors that indicate a person may be intending to attempt suicide. Like other medical warning signs, action is required. NIMH states, "Risk factors are important to keep in

Searching for a gun is a warning sign of suicide. One way to lower someone's risk of suicide is to limit access to firearms.

mind; however, someone who has *warning signs* of suicide may be in more danger and require immediate attention."[16] According to the National Suicide Prevention Lifeline, warning signs of suicide include looking for a way to kill oneself, such as searching online about suicide or buying a gun. Talking about a desire to die or kill oneself, feeling hopeless or having no reason to live, feeling trapped or in unbearable pain, and the perception of being a burden to others are warning signs, too. People who are considering suicide might act anxious or agitated, behave recklessly, sleep too little or too much, show rage or talk about seeking revenge, have extreme mood swings, withdraw or isolate themselves, or increase their use of alcohol or drugs.

The Center for Substance Abuse Treatment says,

Determining with accuracy who will die by suicide using tests or clinical judgment is extremely difficult, if not impossible. . . .

Although precisely who may die by suicide cannot be known, suicide risk assessment is a valuable clinical tool because it can ensure that those requiring more services get the help that they need. In other words, it is not necessary to have a crystal ball if the assessment information shows that a client fits the profile of an individual at significant risk. In such instances, appropriate actions should be taken.[17]

"Although precisely who may die by suicide cannot be known, suicide risk assessment is a valuable clinical tool because it can ensure that those requiring more services get the help that they need."[17]

—Center for Substance Abuse Treatment

Knowledge of risk factors and warning signs can help prevent suicide. The National Suicide Prevention Lifeline is available at 1-800-273-TALK (8255) or online for those who need help.

HOW DOES SUICIDE AFFECT TEENS?

S uicide is complex. Because of the large variety of risk factors, suicidal behavior may manifest in different ways for different people. However, there are certain warning signs people can watch for in themselves or others. If teens spot these warning signs, they can seek help.

Many of the physical and emotional warning signs of suicide are similar to symptoms of depression. Signs that a teen might be struggling include emotional changes, such as worrying often, feeling deeply sad or hopeless, and becoming easily irritable or angry. Physical changes can vary, but they include feeling tired all the time and having headaches, dizziness, chest pain, or stomachaches. Someone may also show changes in sleeping and eating habits, sleeping or eating more or less than usual. Other clues to mental health issues and suicidality can be

There are many physical signs that a teen is overwhelmed. For example, a teen may have frequent headaches and stomachaches.

seen when someone's social interaction, behavior, and activity level change. Teens might express less interest in spending time with friends or doing the activities they once enjoyed. They might lose interest in school or have trouble focusing. Teens might also turn to alcohol, drugs, or self-harm.

Some warning signs show a more serious threat and may require immediate intervention. These include someone threatening or looking for ways to hurt or kill himself, someone looking for pills or weapons, or someone talking or writing about death or suicide. These may be obvious, like someone saying "I'm going to kill myself." However, they could be more subtle signs of suicidal behavior. Someone might say things like, "I'm not going to be a problem anymore," or, "If something happens to me, I want you to know . . ." Someone might begin giving away her favorite possessions or writing a will. Or someone might write a suicide note. All of these signs should be taken seriously. If you see these signs, do not leave the person alone. Call 911 or a trusted adult, or ask someone to make the call for you so you can stay with the person. People having suicidal thoughts can reach out to the National Suicide Prevention Lifeline at 1-800-275-TALK (8255). For people not comfortable talking on the phone, the crisis text line is available. By texting HOME to 741741, texters will be connected with a crisis counselor.

KNOWING WHEN TO GET HELP

When a teen is feeling emotionally overwhelmed or is unable to deal with a difficult situation, it may be time to seek help. Stigma about mental illness can make it hard ask for help, but this step is one of the most important keys to preventing suicide. The APA states, "Currently, the most effective suicide prevention programs equip mental health professionals and other community educators and leaders with sufficient resources to recognize who is at risk and who has access to mental

There are many ways to reach out for help. For example, teens can call a crisis hotline or talk to a trusted adult.

health care."[18] If signs of a mental health disorder are recognized, then professional help is needed.

The AAP encourages seeking help when feeling overwhelmed:

[Asking for help] does not mean you are crazy or a failure. Strong people turn to others for support when they have too much to handle. It's OK to turn to wise friends for

> "[Asking for help] does not mean you are crazy or a failure. Strong people turn to others for support when they have too much to handle. It's OK to turn to wise friends for advice, but it is also important to turn to your parents or another adult to help you."[19]
>
> —*American Academy of Pediatrics*

advice, but it is also important to turn to your parents or another adult to help you. Nobody will solve your problems; they might just help you figure out how to better deal with them. You deserve to feel good.[19]

In a 2018 *New York Times* article, college football player Isaiah Woods discussed how he had dealt with depression and suicide attempts. Woods received a full-ride scholarship to play football for the University of Washington. But the pressures of being part of a major football program began to take their toll. Woods fought against anxiety and feelings of emptiness. He attempted suicide twice within three months. Woods thought he had to be strong and use willpower to deal with his issues. He was afraid his teammates would see him as weak. But his mother and coaches were worried about him, and they encouraged him to see a psychologist. Therapy and medication helped Woods, as did leaving football behind and finding a new path. He now speaks out against the stigma of mental illness. In a 2019 follow-up article, Woods said, "It really helps to feel like the story of my journey has been helpful to people going through some of the same things. The kinds of issues I've faced

There are many online communities where suicide-attempt survivors can connect. On these websites, people can share and listen to stories.

are never anything someone should be ashamed of. I want to be part of that change."[20]

SURVIVORS OF ATTEMPTED SUICIDE

The vast majority of people who have attempted suicide yet survived will not die from suicide. Though survivors may feel alone and ashamed, some receive medical attention, treatment, and counseling for mental health disorders for the first time

SELF-HARM AND SUICIDE

Nonsuicidal self-injury is defined as having caused intentional harm to oneself to soothe emotional pain at least once. This may include cutting or burning oneself. One in five teens have self-injured, according to survey data from more than ten American universities. Self-injury is not the same as suicide. However, research suggests that those who self-harm on a continual basis have a higher risk for suicide.

Self-injury is linked to a history of trauma, such as sexual abuse and other mental illnesses. Self-injury is more often associated with girls and women, but 30 to 40 percent of people who have self-injured are male. According to Janis Whitlock, a researcher at Cornell University, people who self-harm do it as a coping mechanism for anxiety and depression. In an interview with *Time* magazine, Whitlock explained that people who self-harm typically feel one of two ways: numb and disconnected, or overwhelmed with emotion.

In 2019, research explored the connection between physical pain and emotional pain relief. Researchers reported a reduction in self-injury behavior with a specialized therapy called dialectical behavior therapy (DBT). A DBT-trained therapist helps patients recognize upsetting feelings or actions and respond to emotional situations in healthier ways.

after an attempt. Other survivors receive a more accurate diagnosis and better treatment to prevent suicide.

Pediatrician Stephanie Doupnik is an assistant professor of pediatrics at the University of Pennsylvania. She and some colleagues conducted a research study, which she wrote about for Vox. The researchers interviewed twenty-seven teens who were in the emergency room for suicidal thoughts or behaviors. Doupnik wrote,

Sometimes, people who aren't familiar with caring for teenagers at risk of suicide worry

that there is nothing they can do to help if a teen is determined to die. Resoundingly, teenagers expressed just the opposite. They wanted help so that they could stop feeling like they wanted to die. And many of them told us that by coming to the emergency room, they found exactly that— they felt safe. . . . Even before they started specific mental health treatments, just being in a supportive environment helped improve their mental health status.[21]

However, patients in the studies did share their fears. Several patients told researchers they were having "feelings of guilt, remorse, or embarrassment about their suicidal crisis."[22] They also expressed concerns over the next steps of treatment and the return to their daily lives.

COLLEGE SUICIDE POLICIES

Colleges and universities vary in leave policies for students regarding mental illness and suicide attempts. In 2018, students who had been forced to leave Stanford University following a suicide attempt filed a lawsuit against the university. Maia Goddell, supervising attorney for Disability Rights Advocates, said Stanford encouraged students to leave campus as a "first resort" rather than providing the mental health resources to allow students to continue their education. Subsequently, the university revised its leave policy. Students will no longer be encouraged to leave the campus, and they can receive disability accommodation to stay in school. Students can also petition to continue to live in campus housing while on leave, which was already possible for students with medical disabilities. Advocates called the settlement a landmark case and hope other universities will follow suit.

Doupnik emphasized the importance of having a support system to help combat these fears. She said that while teens who have had a suicidal crisis are at a higher risk of experiencing another one, getting treatment allows most teens to get the help they need to recover.

Dese'Rae L. Stage knows the importance of having support. As a suicide survivor, she had searched for support online and couldn't find any. She explains,

> I did some research. I Googled 'suicide survivor,' and what I found was people who had lost someone they loved, not people like me, who had tried to die and lived instead—people who were confused about what happened next, who felt so much shame that they couldn't talk about what had happened to them, people who felt misunderstood and alone. I didn't know what kind of language I should use to even try to find those people. There were no resources for attempt survivors. I decided that this was where I would focus my efforts.[23]

"I Googled 'suicide survivor,' and what I found was people who had lost someone they loved, not people like me, who had tried to die and lived instead—people who were confused about what happened next, who felt so much shame that they couldn't talk about what had happened to them, people who felt misunderstood and alone. . . . There were no resources for attempt survivors."[23]

—Dese'Rae L. Stage, founder of
Live Through This

Stage founded the Live Through This suicide prevention effort. The website features first-person accounts of suicide-attempt survivors accompanied by portraits taken by Stage, who travels around the country to interview and photograph the survivors. Stage hopes these true stories and portraits of people of all ages and experiences provide comfort, compassion, understanding, and hope for people affected by suicide.

LOSING SOMEONE TO SUICIDE

Losing a loved one to suicide is a devastating experience. People who have lost someone to suicide may experience ongoing pain and suffering, including grief, depression, anxiety, PTSD, and increased risk of suicidal thoughts and suicide, according to the CDC.

Those grieving loss from suicide often face different challenges than others facing loss. Grievers may fear stigma, shame, or isolation if they discuss the suicide. Tensions can rise in families when those left behind disagree about how to discuss the victim's death. Others may be spurred to advocacy by a loved one's suicide, speaking out in hopes of helping others.

People who have lost someone to suicide may feel mixed emotions. They may feel anger or abandonment toward the victim, while others may turn to self-blame, thinking they should have been able to stop it. Clinical psychologist Jack Jordan explained that the grief following suicide is life-changing: "Suicide

Suicide support groups exist for those who have lost friends and family members to suicide. People can feel connected through sharing their experiences.

can shatter the things you take for granted about yourself, your relationships, and your world."[24] Loved ones may cope by learning as much as they can about the factors and situations that led to the suicide. Sometimes they will ask the same questions again and again.

> "Suicide can shatter the things you take for granted about yourself, your relationships, and your world."[24]
>
> —*Jack Jordan, clinical psychologist*

Mental health professionals, suicide support groups, and friends can provide support by being good listeners.

The holiday season can be an especially difficult time for people experiencing suicide loss. Each year, the International Survivors of Suicide Loss Day takes place on the Saturday before Thanksgiving in the United States. The day was created from a resolution introduced by former US Senator Harry Reid of Nevada. Reid's father died from suicide, and Reid is a longtime champion of suicide prevention efforts.

Suicide affects different people in different ways. Those who experience suicidal ideation or behavior, those who have survived suicide attempts, and those who have lost loved ones to suicide all struggle in different ways. But with help and support, people who are affected by suicide can overcome its effects.

CHAPTER THREE

HOW IS TEEN SUICIDE RELATED TO SOCIETY?

I t might seem strange to think of behavior as contagious, but there is strong evidence of contagion occurring with suicide. A contagion is usually defined as a disease that can be passed from one person to another by touching. Suicide contagion refers to the increased risk of suicide resulting from direct or indirect exposure to suicide or suicidal behaviors. Direct exposure happens when a close contact dies by suicide, such as a family member, friend, neighbor, coworker, coach, or teacher. Indirect exposure refers to a secondhand account of suicide, such as a news story, social media post, or fictional story. Teens and young adults are especially affected by both direct and indirect accounts through their social networks. In the United States, 33 percent of people have known someone who

Suicide contagion happens when a suicide death is caused by exposure to another suicide. Exposure to suicide can be direct and indirect.

has died from suicide. Experts say that after a suicide, a mental health evaluation and treatment can minimize suicide risk in the individual's family members, friends, peers, and colleagues.

According to the American Association of Suicidology, the suicide deaths of celebrities often contribute to suicide contagion as well as increased suicide prevention awareness. The public frequently identifies with well-known people, and stories about their suicides are reported widely and for a long time. Actor and comedian Robin Williams died from suicide on August 11, 2014. Calls to the National Suicide Prevention Lifeline increased 300 percent and suicide rates increased significantly within thirty days of his suicide. Visits to the Suicide Prevention Resource Center and Suicide Awareness Voices of Education websites also increased. Media contagion from celebrity suicide and general suicide coverage have been carefully studied. According to the Reporting on Suicide initiative, "More than 50 research studies worldwide have found that certain types of news coverage can increase the likelihood of suicide in vulnerable individuals. The magnitude of the increase is related to the amount, duration, and prominence of coverage."[25]

A suicide cluster describes an unusually high rate of suicides, usually in a specific geographic location or during a

MEDIA STANDARDS FOR REPORTING ON SUICIDE

Covering suicide carefully can encourage those who are at risk of suicide to seek help. Suicide is the result of many complex factors; reporting should avoid oversimplified explanations such as recent negative life events or stressors. Coverage should inform the audience without sensationalizing the suicide and minimize glorification by not using dramatic headlines or graphic images. Reports should not reveal detailed descriptions of the method used to avoid possible copycat suicide. Coverage should focus on suicide as a public health issue—not as a crime. Suicide prevention experts should be sought for advice on reporting. In addition, information such as hotlines or emergency contacts should be provided for those at risk for suicide.

Actor and comedian Robin Williams died by suicide in 2014. When a celebrity dies by suicide, it may spread suicide contagion.

specific time. Following the release of the Netflix series *13 Reasons Why*, suicide contagion and clusters were suspected and noted by mental health professionals and emergency room doctors, and these early reports were later confirmed by multiple research findings. Researchers have also examined social media's role. They have looked at a three-month window of peak activity about *13 Reasons Why* on Instagram and Twitter,

CTE

Researchers hypothesize that concussions lead to chronic traumatic encephalopathy (CTE), which is prevalent in NFL players. The symptoms of CTE include irritability, aggression, mood swings, depression, suicidal thoughts, memory loss, and cognitive problems. Substance abuse and a high rate of suicide have also been reported in the early stages of CTE. In its most advanced form, CTE is hard to distinguish from Alzheimer's disease, which is characterized by loss of memory. CTE tends to manifest in two ways. Early-age onset occurs at age thirty-five or younger and includes behavioral and mood changes. Late-age onset occurs around age sixty and includes severe effects on brain functioning and memory. However, recent studies conclude that the link between CTE and suicide results from a phenomena called "selection bias." Because the suicide of an NFL player is reported in the media, people overestimate its occurrence and make a connection to CTE.

which coincided with increased suicides. Two more research groups, one looking at national data and the other at community data, found the suicide rate in preteens and teens had increased in the time period after the release of the series in April 2017. In contrast, researchers observed no significant increases in suicides among older age groups after the series' release.

The researchers of one 2019 study explained that stories on suicide, real and fictional, are affecting children and teens.

"Caution must be taken in interpreting these findings; however, the suicide increase in youth only and the signal of a potentially larger increase in young females all appear to be consistent with a contagion by media and seem to reinforce the need for collaboration toward improving fictional portrayals of suicide."[26]

Portrayals of suicide can have a positive impact on viewers, depending on the context. Depicting a mental health condition accurately, as well as showing and writing characters in books, film, and television who seek help and overcome a suicidal crisis, are all linked to positive impacts. "It is helpful to convey a message that change is possible, even in seemingly desperate circumstances," the WHO says.[27] These accounts could be used to protect against suicide and reduce stigma.

> "It is helpful to convey a message that change is possible, even in seemingly desperate circumstances."[27]
>
> **—World Health Organization**

STIGMA OF MENTAL ILLNESS

Differences in cultural backgrounds can affect attitudes toward mental illness and suicide. The stigma of mental illness has a long history, and many cultures share it in some form. An example of a cultural taboo related to suicide is the belief that asking if someone is suicidal could cause it to happen. In reality, talking about suicide reduces the stigma of mental illness. Bernice Pescosolido, a professor

> "In the 1950s, you never told anybody you had cancer. Many problems have gone through this, and we've made progress on others. Issues with the mind, and the brain, and personal relationships are the last frontier. They're the last thing we need to learn how to talk about."[28]
>
> **—Bernice Pescosolido, professor of sociology**

Stigma around suicide may make people feel shame. Having open conversations about mental health and suicide can reduce this stigma.

of sociology at Indiana University, told the *Atlantic* that stigma of cancer was once similar to that of suicide today. "In the 1950s, you never told anybody you had cancer. Many problems have gone through this, and we've made progress on others. Issues with the mind, and the brain, and personal relationships are the last frontier. They're the last thing we need to learn how to talk about."[28]

Attitudes toward cancer evolved as a result of public health initiatives in the 1970s and 1980s. Campaigns today hope to change attitudes about mental health in a similar way. The Make It OK campaign aims to reduce the stigma of mental illness and help people to think of mental illness in the same way they now think of cancer. Online classes explore mental illness and stigma. On the Make It OK website, people are asked to sign a pledge to reduce stigma and share it on social media.

FIRST RESPONDERS AND SUICIDE

Law enforcement officers are often the first responders on the scene of attempted suicides and suicides. When law enforcement responds to a suicide or suicide attempt call, the officers secure the scene, assess the person for medical treatment, and build trust with the person to check for suicide risk. Officers look for toxic substances, alcohol, drugs, or medications that might have been taken. If the person is in imminent danger, the officers will arrange for transport to the hospital or a mental health center. If the person refuses to be transported, law enforcement can issue a seventy-two-hour hold for evaluation at a mental health facility in most states. Some police departments receive specialized training from mental health professionals for appropriate suicide response. Other departments partner with mental health providers and community advocates in responding to a suicide call. This group of professionals is called a crisis intervention team.

Law enforcement is trained to help those at imminent risk of suicide. The police may place a suicide-attempt survivor in a mental health facility.

Kevin Briggs, a state trooper in San Francisco, recounted his experience saving people from suicide attempts. In his time responding to suicide attempts on the Golden Gate Bridge, he was able to save all but two people. Briggs and his fellow Marin County officers are trained in how to intervene when someone is feeling suicidal, connect to those in crisis, and stop a suicide.

During his twenty-three years patrolling the bridge, Briggs learned that stepping in and helping the person to see that they have other choices are key to preventing suicide: "By just being there, you may just be the turning point that they need. If you think someone is suicidal, don't be afraid to confront them and ask the question. One way of asking them the question is like this: 'Others in similar circumstances have thought about ending their life; have you had these thoughts?' Confronting the person head-on may just save their life and be the turning point for them."[29]

> "By just being there, you may just be the turning point that they need. If you think someone is suicidal, don't be afraid to confront them and ask the question. . . . Confronting the person head-on may just save their life and be the turning point for them."[29]
>
> —*Kevin Briggs, state trooper*

CHAPTER FOUR

HOW CAN WE PREVENT TEEN SUICIDE?

Public health organizations are developing, implementing, and evaluating strategies to prevent suicide. The government, communities, employers, schools, health care systems, the media, and individuals can contribute to this goal, according to the CDC. The federal government tracks suicide trends and identifies at-risk groups, and communities offer activities for people to feel connected. Employers apply policies that reduce stigma about seeking help, schools teach coping and problem-solving skills, and health care systems train providers in effective treatments for patients at risk of suicide. Everyone can help prevent suicide by learning the warning signs and taking appropriate action when someone is at risk of suicide.

The government, employers, schools, and other communities can all work together to prevent suicide. One of the first steps is recognizing the warning signs.

GLOBAL PUBLIC HEALTH EFFORT ON SUICIDE

In 2013, global targets to reduce suicide were set by the WHO and the United Nations (UN). The WHO aimed for a 10 percent reduction in suicide by 2020. By 2030, the UN targeted a reduction in the suicide rate by one-third. WHO recommended the following four interventions to help achieve these goals. First, identify as early as possible those who are thinking about suicide or who have made a suicide attempt and keep follow-up contact. Second, restrict access to means of suicide, such as firearms. Third, help people develop skills to cope with life's pressures. Finally, work with the media to ensure responsible reporting of suicide.

MENTAL HEALTH ASSESSMENT AND FINDING A MENTAL HEALTH PROFESSIONAL

One proven prevention strategy is to focus on the early identification and treatment of people with known risk factors for suicide: those with mental illness, substance use disorders, chronic pain, and emotional distress. The APA recommends taking the following steps to prevent suicide in teens: get treatment for any underlying mental health issues, receive adequate sleep each night, limit alcohol and substance use, and learn coping skills and resilience to deal with stress.

Taking steps to get treatment for mental health issues can feel harder than getting medical treatment for a physical wound. One way to combat the stigma of mental illness is to increase the transparency about how mental health treatment works, as well as removing barriers to seeking and receiving treatment. The organization Screening for Mental Health, Inc. (SMH) focuses on

WAYS TO PREVENT SUICIDE

RESTRICTING ACCESS TO MEANS
Limit the availability of firearms and lethal substances by placing them in safe or locked areas.

RESPONSIBLE MEDIA REPORTING
The media should not glorify suicide or use language that blames the victim. The media should be conscious of suicide contagion.

INTRODUCING ALCOHOL POLICIES
Statewide policies, such as limiting liquor store density and raising taxes on alcohol, are ways to reduce heavy alcohol use.

EFFECTIVE MEASURES

EARLY IDENTIFICATION AND TREATMENT
Use screening tools that identify the level of emotional stress someone feels. Make appointments with primary care doctors, who can refer to mental health care professionals.

FOLLOW-UP CARE AND COMMUNITY SUPPORT
Continue visiting mental health care professionals. Get involved in communities and organizations that offer support, such as the National Institute for Mental Health (NIMH).

TRAINING OF HEALTH WORKERS
Health care workers take courses to perform accurate suicide assessments and safety planning procedures.

These prevention strategies are recommended by the World Health Organization (WHO). The organization helps people get health coverage and protects people from mental health emergencies.

People can determine if they need help by taking an online mental health questionnaire. This involves questions about someone's stress and pain levels.

making it easier for teens and young adults to get help for mental health issues by offering an online tool to determine if they would benefit from treatment. The organization also offers in-person visits to a health care professional for an assessment. During a mental health assessment, the health care provider will ask a series of questions. These questions help the provider assess someone's stress and emotional pain levels as well as her mental health history. Following the assessment, the provider develops a treatment plan with the patient. Treatment often involves many strategies such as counseling, medications, support groups, and educational programs. SMH also explains how therapy is not only a crisis strategy but also a long-term maintenance and prevention strategy: "Mental health treatment is an ongoing process that can be crucial to supporting people during intense times of crisis. Mental health treatment can also be very beneficial to help maintain good mental health over time."[30]

When seeking mental health treatment for a teen, parents can take a team approach, involving medical professionals, schools, trusted friends and family, and support organizations. A primary care physician is a good starting point for help with diagnosis, treatment, and possible referral to a mental health professional.

Mental health professional is a general term for those who work in the mental health field. In the United States, mental health professionals need to meet certain requirements set by each state to receive a license to treat patients. Only certain mental health professionals can prescribe medications to their patients. Psychiatrists and primary care physicians have a medical school degree, so they can prescribe medication. Many states also allow nurse practitioners and psychiatric pharmacists to prescribe medication. Psychologists, social workers, therapists, and counselors cannot prescribe medication.

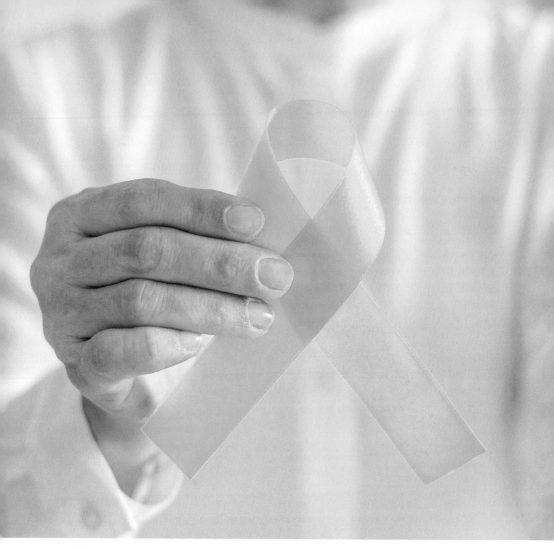

Many organizations exist to spread suicide awareness. A yellow ribbon represents suicide prevention.

This group of professionals can make assessments and diagnoses and provide individual and group therapy. They often work in medical clinic and office settings.

Zero Suicide is a health care–based program, first launched in the United Kingdom, to identify and care for those who may be at risk of suicide. The program started with the realization that

83 percent of people who die by suicide have seen a health care professional in the preceding year, whereas only 29 percent had seen a behavioral health specialist. To Steve Mallen, founder of the Zero Suicide program, this statistic pointed to a failure in the health care system framework. To fix it, he believed the health care system needed to make an organization-wide commitment to suicide prevention as an essential responsibility. People at risk for suicide were seen in the health care system, but they did not receive comprehensive care to prevent suicide. Zero Suicide aims to identify patients before a suicidal crisis. The early results of this program have been impressive, and interest in replicating these results is growing. For example, the Henry Ford Health System demonstrated a 75 percent reduction in the suicide rate among their health plan members with the Zero Suicide program. Similarly, Centerstone, one of the largest behavioral health providers in the United States, reported a decrease of suicide deaths from thirty-five per 100,000 to thirteen per 100,000 three years after initiating the program.

For Mallen, the program is fulfilling a promise to his son, who died from suicide in 2015. Mallen said in an interview with *Mosaic Science,*

> *My son was dying in front of me and I couldn't see it, despite my education, despite my devotion as a father. . . . So you see this is coming from an incredible*

sense of guilt. I suppose what I'm trying to do is save my boy in retrospect. I stood next to his coffin in the church. It was packed with people—a shattered community—and I made him a public promise. I said that I would investigate what had happened to him and that I would seek reform for him, and on behalf of his generation.[31]

TREATMENT WITH THERAPY

Cognitive behavioral therapy (CBT) and dialectical behavioral therapy (DBT) are two types of psychotherapy that are effective for preventing suicide in at-risk individuals. CBT focuses on thought patterns and helps a person consider alternative actions when thoughts of suicide arise. There are three common phases in CBT. During phase one, the therapist might ask the patient to tell a story about his or her most recent suicidal thought or behavior. During the second phase, the therapist and patient discuss how to regulate emotions tied to things that might trigger suicidal thoughts. During this phase, someone might learn how to regulate self-hatred. The third phase is typically characterized by prevention strategies. Since relapse, or the reoccurrence of suicidal ideation, is common, this phase is key to helping the patient. This tends to give patients more confidence in handling emotional regulation before a crisis occurs.

DBT focuses on regulating emotions and using healthy coping skills to change behavior. Dialectics is the idea that opposing forces can coexist. According to clinical psychologist Esme Shaller, "We often think of dialectics as a great big scale, tilting back and forth. The main dialectic in DBT is that we are always trying to balance acceptance (you're doing the best you can . . .) with change (you have to try different things to get the life you want)."[32] DBT works with patients on mindfulness practice,

FIVE STEPS FOR HELPING SOMEONE IN EMOTIONAL PAIN

NIMH's website features a list of five steps that concerned people can use when a person they care about is going through difficult times. These steps can make a difference in preventing suicide. First, someone can ask the person if he or she is thinking about suicide. This can be a difficult conversation to start. But the evidence shows that simply asking the question does not increase the chances of suicide. Second, someone can keep the person safe by restricting his or her access to lethal items, such as firearms, medications, and hazardous locations. Third, someone can be present with the person, listening carefully to learn what he or she is thinking and feeling. Acknowledging and talking about suicide may reduce suicidal thoughts in at-risk people, according to research studies. Fourth, someone can help the person connect with a family member, friend, mental health professional, or religious advisor. Fifth, someone can stay connected with the person after a crisis or after being released from a health care setting. Follow-up reduces the number of deaths by suicide, according to research studies. For additional help, the National Suicide Prevention Lifeline can be accessed at 1-800-273-TALK (8255).

interpersonal effectiveness skills, emotion regulation skills, and distress tolerance skills. Therapy may include both individual therapy and group therapy to learn new coping skills.

A collaborative care team approach with primary care doctors and mental health specialists is also recommended by Zero Suicide. The team, with the patient, decides on a treatment plan. It might include medication in addition to therapy. In addition, Attachment-Based Family Therapy (ABFT) is a treatment supported for suicidal teens. ABFT focuses on family dynamics by building meaningful relationships. Children with healthy attachments to parents and caretakers are more likely to be able to regulate their emotions.

Safety planning has also been shown to reduce suicidal thoughts and behavior. Patients work with a therapist to make a personalized safety plan to consult when in a crisis. The safety plan describes ways to reduce access to lethal means, lists coping strategies, and includes contact information for designated emergency contacts. According to NIMH, when at-risk patients also receive a series of supportive phone calls, their risk of suicide decreases. Therapists often pair a no-suicide agreement with safety planning, called *Contract for Safety*. The patient typically makes a written agreement not to harm him- or herself.

Attachment-Based Family Therapy focuses on building strong family relationships. It is important for suicidal teens to have a support system.

PREVENTION IN SCHOOLS

High schools, colleges, and universities are important parts of suicide awareness, education, and prevention efforts. In October 2019, the first Model School Policy on Suicide Prevention was

Different types of therapy can help someone reduce her risk of suicide. CBT is one helpful intervention for teens.

published by the American Foundation for Suicide Prevention, in collaboration with the American School Counselor Association, the National Association of School Psychologists, and the Trevor Project. It provides guidance on implementation of suicide-related policies in US schools. The model school policy covers suicide prevention by identifying at-risk students and working with parents and guardians. The policy also covers intervention by training teachers in procedures for responding to students who attempt suicide at school. Lastly, the policy covers postvention, which involves the school's response and procedures following a suicide in the school community. Stop a Suicide Today is a school-based suicide prevention program that is responsible for a documented reduction in self-reported suicide attempts. Developed by Harvard psychiatrist Douglas Jacobs, Stop a Suicide Today teaches people how to recognize the signs of suicide and to take action.

Many colleges and universities have counseling

HELPFUL MEDICATION

Ketamine, a drug approved by the US Food and Drug Administration (FDA) in 1970, is considered a possible treatment for suicidal thoughts and behavior. It has long been used for pain relief, primarily in patients with severe burns. The drug's potential to offer fast relief for severe depression is a more recent discovery. Unfortunately, ketamine has serious side effects, such as psychosis and dissociation, or feeling detached from one's body. Another downside is the problem of illegal use of ketamine.

Researchers are working to develop ketamine-like drugs that act on a similar part of the brain as ketamine, but are more precisely targeted to avoid its side effects. Ketamine-like drugs have received "breakthrough therapy designation" from the FDA, which means the therapy shows promise to improve the outcome of a serious or life-threatening condition and its approval will be fast-tracked by the government. These drugs appear to relieve the symptoms of severe depression and stop suicidal thoughts and behavior.

centers to address the mental health needs of students. Nathan Pointer, a suicide-attempt survivor featured on the Live Through This website, shared his experience at his university. Pointer explained, "I came in to the school with this diagnosis and with this set of expectations and with a need for medication, and they got right on it. They put me in with a doctor to manage my medication and they got me into counseling—which I had never really been in before—right away, with a great counselor . . . . They have done an excellent job of serving me personally."[33]

REDUCING ACCESS TO LETHAL MEANS

Researchers found that storing firearms unloaded, separate from ammunition, and in a locked place or secured with a safety device was protective against suicide attempts among adolescents. "Another important step in suicide prevention is to lock up and safely store any firearms in your home as these can be lethal in an impulsive situation," write Ana Radovic and Megan A. Moreno in *JAMA Pediatrics*.[34] According to Zero Suicide, reducing access to lethal means can save lives. Many suicide attempts occur with little to

"Another important step in suicide prevention is to lock up and safely store any firearms in your home as these can be lethal in an impulsive situation."[34]

—Ana Radovic and Megan A. Moreno, mental health professionals

Easy access to firearms increases risk of suicide. Guns and other lethal items should be kept in a secure area.

no planning, and the firearms used in teen suicide usually belong to a parent.

People can reduce access to firearms by relying on an extreme risk protection order (ERPO). ERPOs are issued by

Social support is key for those at risk of suicide. Having caring friends, parents, and mentors decreases someone's risk of suicide.

courts to keep people who are at risk of hurting themselves or others from buying or having guns. Studies of ERPOs in Connecticut and Indiana suggest that these orders are effective at preventing suicide. According to sociologist Jeffrey Swanson, "In Connecticut and Indiana, researchers like me found that for every 10 to 20 gun-removal actions under such laws, one life was saved through an averted suicide."[35] In 2019, many states and the District of Columbia now have ERPO laws in place.

TEACHING COPING SKILLS

Coping strategies help with stress by relieving uncomfortable feelings such as fear, worry, anger, frustration, or grief. A coping strategy is anything that makes someone feel better in response to stress. Healthy coping strategies deal with the problem, use self-care, and allow for an emotional response. Exercise, meditation, prayer, creative pursuits, journaling, crying, laughing, helping others, talking with trusted friends or family, and listening to music are examples of positive ways to cope with stress.

Teaching coping skills using social-emotional learning programs in schools is highly effective in reducing both suicide and severe suicidal thoughts among teens. Social-emotional learning programs teach self-awareness, emotional monitoring, and social skills. The Youth Aware of Mental Health (YAM) program is designed for teenagers ages fourteen to sixteen. It uses role-playing and interactive discussions to teach adolescents about the risk and protective factors associated with suicide. For example, a role-play might involve showing empathy when responding to a friend who is feeling depressed. The YAM program enhances teens' problem-solving skills for dealing with stress, school, and other problems. YAM was developed and tested in Europe. In a study conducted across ten EU countries and 168 schools, students who used YAM were significantly less likely to attempt suicide and have severe suicidal thoughts at one-year follow-up compared with students in the control group schools. Students in the control group schools only received educational materials about suicide.

People who have supportive friends and family are more likely to stay in treatment, cope with daily difficulties, and rely on others in a crisis. The Youth-Nominated Support Team Intervention for Suicidal Adolescents studied the impact of social support on suicide prevention in at-risk teens. This intervention provides training to adult supportive contacts for teens who have been hospitalized for suicide risk. The teen gets to choose supportive adults to serve as contacts for ongoing help and support. Data from this clinical trial were reported in 2019, more than a decade after the trial started. Suicide deaths were significantly reduced in the support team group compared to the control group, which had received standard treatment.

"Research indicates that suicide risk changes as a result of the number and intensity of key risk and protective factors experienced. Ideally, the availability of multiple strategies and approaches tailored to the social, economic, cultural, and environmental context of individuals and communities . . . may increase the likelihood of removing barriers to supportive and effective care."[34]

—CDC

LOWERING SUICIDE RISK

Prevention strategies offer protection against suicide risk, much like a vaccination protects someone against future exposure to a sickness. According to the CDC, "Research

Books, films, and TV shows can help with suicide prevention efforts. One way the media can do this is by showing characters reaching out to get help for mental health issues.

indicates that suicide risk changes as a result of the number and intensity of key risk and protective factors experienced. Ideally, the availability of multiple strategies and approaches tailored

The Friendship Bench is one worldwide effort to reduce suicide. It encourages people to reach out for help.

to the social, economic, cultural, and environmental context of individuals and communities . . . may increase the likelihood of removing barriers to supportive and effective care."[36]

Worldwide, people are making headway to reduce deaths by suicide. One inspiring effort is "The Friendship Bench." Dr. Dixon Chibanda lost a patient from suicide and decided to focus his efforts on treating depression in Zimbabwe. According to the

New York Times, the benches are an effective and accessible treatment for depression. Nurses and staff receive training in talk therapy for depression and suicidality. When clinic staff sees someone on the bench, they leave the clinic to help them by having a conversation. The program started in 2006. By 2020, there were benches outside every Harare government-run clinic and more throughout Zimbabwe and other African countries. New York is trying a similar approach. "I started to realize that psychiatry in an institution is not the way to go," Chibanda told the *New York Times*. "We have to take it to the community."[37]

> "I started to realize that psychiatry in an institution is not the way to go. We have to take it to the community."[37]
>
> —*Dixon Chibanda, psychiatrist*

Suicide is a problem that affects countless teens in different ways. But there is hope to stop it. Responsible media reporting, reducing mental health stigma, and identifying risk factors and warning signs all play a role in stopping suicide.

SOURCE NOTES

INTRODUCTION: SUICIDE IN THE MEDIA

1. Thomas Niederkrotenthaler et al., "Association of Increased Youth Suicides in the United States with the Release of *13 Reasons Why*," *JAMA Psychiatry*, May 29, 2019. www.jamanetwork.com.

2. Quoted in "'13 Reasons Why' and Young Adults' Risk of Suicide," *EurekAlert!*, April 25, 2019. www.eurekalert.org.

3. "Preventing Suicide: A Resource for Media Professionals, Update 2017," *World Health Organization*, 2017. www.who.int.

4. "Fact Sheets: Suicide," *World Health Organization*, September 2, 2019. www.who.int.

CHAPTER 1: WHAT IS SUICIDE?

5. John Ackerman, Elizabeth Cannon, Dese'Rae Stage, et al., "Suicide Reporting Recommendations: Media as Partners in Suicide Prevention," *American Association of Suicidology*, 2018. http://suicidology.org.

6. "Preventing Suicide: A Resource for Media Professionals."

7. *Merriam-Webster Online*, s.v. "commit," February 28, 2020. www.merriam-webster.com.

8. Ackerman et al., "Suicide Reporting Recommendations."

9. Quoted in Gerry Holt, "When Suicide Was Illegal," *BBC News*, August 3, 2011. www.bbc.com.

10. Benjamin Shain, "Suicide and Suicide Attempts in Adolescents," *American Academy of Pediatrics*, July 2016. http://pediatrics.aappublications.org.

11. Deb Stone et al., "Preventing Suicide: A Technical Package of Policy, Programs, and Practices," *Centers for Disease Control and Prevention*, 2017. www.cdc.gov.

12. "Suicide in America: Frequently Asked Questions," *National Institutes of Mental Health*, n.d. www.nimh.nih.gov.

13. "Suicide Rising Across the US," *Centers for Disease Control and Prevention*, June 7, 2018. www.cdc.gov.

14. Quoted in "Talking About Suicide and LGBT Populations," *The Trevor Project*, 2011. www.thetrevorproject.org.

15. Joan Luby and Sarah Kertz, "Increasing Suicide Rates in Early Adolescent Girls in the United States and the Equalization of Sex Disparity in Suicide: The Need to Investigate the Role of Social Media," *JAMA Network*, May 17, 2019. www.jamanetwork.com.

16. "Suicide in America: Frequently Asked Questions."

17. Center for Substance Abuse Treatment, "Addressing Suicidal Thoughts and Behaviors in Substance Abuse Treatment," *Substance Abuse and Mental Health Services Administration*, 2009. www.ncbi.nlm.nih.gov.

CHAPTER 2: HOW DOES SUICIDE AFFECT TEENS?

18. "Teen Suicide Is Preventable," *American Psychological Association*, n.d. www.apa.org.

19. Ed. Kenneth Ginsburg and Sara Kinsman, "Reaching Teens: Strength-Based Communication Strategies to Build Resilience and Support Healthy Adolescent Development," *American Academy of Pediatrics*, 2014. http://ebooks.aapublications.org.

20. Quoted in Kurt Streeter, "A Football Player's Mental Health Struggle Led Him Toward New Ambitions," *New York Times*, December 27, 2019. www.nytimes.com.

21. Stephanie Doupnik, "I Treat Teens Who Attempted Suicide. Here's What They Told Me," *Vox*, November 6, 2019. www.vox.com.

22. Doupnik, "I Treat Teens Who Attempted Suicide."

23. "Dese'Rae L. Stage Is a Suicide Attempt Survivor," *Live Through This*, February 23, 2016. http://livethroughthis.org.

24. Quoted in "Left Behind after Suicide," *Harvard Health*, May 29, 2019. www.health.harvard.edu.

SOURCE NOTES CONTINUED

CHAPTER 3: HOW IS TEEN SUICIDE RELATED TO SOCIETY?

25. "Recommendations for Reporting on Suicide: Important Points for Covering Suicide," *Reporting on Suicide*, n.d. http://reportingonsuicide.org.

26. Niederkrotenthaler et al., "Association of Increased Youth Suicides in the United States with the Release of *13 Reasons Why*."

27. "Preventing Suicide: A Resource for Filmmakers and Others Working on Stage and Screen," *World Health Organization*, 2019. www.who.int.

28. Quoted in Julie Beck, "When Will People Get Better at Talking About Suicide?" *Atlantic*, June 9, 2018. www.theatlantic.com.

29. Kevin Briggs, "The Bridge Between Suicide and Life," *TED*, 2014. www.ted.com.

CHAPTER 4: HOW CAN WE PREVENT TEEN SUICIDE?

30. "Get Help," *Stop a Suicide Today*, n.d. http://stopasuicide.org.

31. Quoted in Simon Usborne, "How to Get to a World Without Suicide," *Mosaic Science*, July 31, 2017. http://mosaicscience.com.

32. Esme Shaller, "What Is DBT?" *DBT Center of Lawrence*, n.d. http://dbtlawrence.com.

33. Quoted in Dese'Rae Stage, "Nathan Pointer Is a Suicide Attempt Survivor," *Live Through This*, April 7, 2014. http://livethroughthis.org.

34. Ana Radovic and Megan A. Moreno, "Treatment Options for Adolescent Depression," *JAMA Pediatrics*, January 28, 2019. www.jamanetwork.com.

35. Jeffrey Swanson, "Red-Flag Laws Thwart Suicides. But Can They Catch Would-Be Mass Killers?" *Washington Post*, August 9, 2019. www.washingtonpost.com.

36. Deb Stone et al., "Preventing Suicide."

37. Quoted in Tina Rosenberg, "Five Who Spread Hope in 2019," *New York Times*, December 17, 2019. www.nytimes.com.

FOR FURTHER RESEARCH

BOOKS

Jennifer Ashton, *Life After Suicide: Finding Courage, Comfort & Community After Unthinkable Loss*. New York: William Morrow, 2019.

Cherese Cartlidge, *Teens and Suicide*. San Diego, CA: ReferencePoint Press, 2017.

Chris Forhan, *My Father Before Me: A Memoir*. New York: Scribner, 2016.

Bradley Steffens, *The Suicide Epidemic*. San Diego, CA: ReferencePoint Press, 2020.

INTERNET SOURCES

Allison Abrams, "The Catastrophic Effects of Mental Health Stigma," *Psychology Today*, May 25, 2017. www.psychology.com.

"NIMH Answers Questions About Suicide," *National Institute of Mental Health*, n.d. www.nimh.nih.gov.

Simon Usborne, "How to Get to a World Without Suicide," *Mosaic Science*, August 1, 2017. www.mosaicscience.com.

WEBSITES

CDC: Suicide Prevention
www.cdc.gov/violenceprevention/suicide/index.html

The CDC website on suicide prevention offers fast facts, community prevention strategies, tips for coping with stress, and more.

Live Through This
https://livethroughthis.org

Established in 2010, the Live Through This website features a collection of portraits and true stories of suicide-attempt survivors across the United States.

National Center for the Prevention of Youth Suicide (NCPYS)
www.preventyouthsuicide.org

The American Association of Suicidology's website for teens offers resources for schools, the LGBTQ community, and more, as well as information about the NCPYS Youth Advisory Board.

Stop a Suicide Today
https://stopasuicide.org

A program of Screening for Mental Health, Inc., this website provides information on getting help for suicide, learning how to help someone with suicidal feelings, and online screening tools for mental health.

INDEX

INDEX CONTINUED

IMAGE CREDITS

ABOUT
THE AUTHOR

Mary Quirk is a freelance writer who loves to read, write, and talk about science. She has worked as a research scientist at the University of Minnesota Medical School and has interned with a science education program on PBS. She teaches after-school science classes for students in Minneapolis, Minnesota, where she lives with her husband and daughter.